R for Beginners: One Rule Predictive Modelling

Djoni Darmawikarta

Contents

Introduction

Welcome to One-Rule Predictive Modeling. It is one of the books in the R Beginners series.

The title of the book speaks for itself: You will learn one-rule predictive modelling in R environment.

In this Introduction to the book, we will cover the following topics briefly.

- Predictive case study used in the examples: Credit card upgrade offer
- What is one-rule predictive model?
- Perquisite skill
- Required software to follow the book exercises

The prediction in the book examples is about credit card upgrade: If we offer an upgrade, we would like to predict whether the cardholder will Accepted or Declined the offer.

What kind of predictive model will we build?

Let's take look at the sample cardholder data in the following table.

In real-life modelling, the number of predictors can more than 25, and the number rows in the order of hundreds of thousands.

CARDHOLDER	CARD	JOB	TRAVEL	MARITAL
Ann	Gold	Admin	Frequent	Divorced
Dee	Silver	Sales	Frequent	Single
Alfonso	Silver	Sales	Occasional	Single
Isaac	Silver	Admin	Rare	Single

We'd like to build a predictive model that can answer the question: Which one of the predictors: Travel Frequency, Marital Status, Current Card Type, or Job Type, will most accurately predicts the target column, the Upgrade Result: Accepted or Declined?

One-rule predictive model can exactly answer that question !

One-rule predictive model selects one of the predictors, the most accurate predictor, and express the prediction in the form of If - Then rules

If the one-rule predictive model finds that TRAVEL is the most accurate predictor, the rules will look like:

```
If TRAVEL = frequent Then UPGRADE = Accepted
If TRAVEL = occasional Then UPGRADE = Declined
If TRAVEL = rare Then UPGRADE = Declined
```

The algorithm, hence the predictive model, is named one-rule as the rule involved only **one** predictor.

One Rule predictive model though looks simple has been proved to be relatively accurate. Read https://link.springer.com/content/pdf/10.1023/A:1022631118932.pdf to appreciate the performance of One Rule model.

Prerequisite skills

In addition to general computer experience, as you will specifically use R, you need to have some R working skills. If you are new to R or needs to refresh your R skill, consult the Appendix of this book and try the examples. The Appendix is located after Chapter 6.

Required Software

To earn the best from the book, try the examples: Type the commands and execute them. If the execution is erroneous or the output is not as expected, investigate, update the commands, and try again.

To try the book examples, you need to have an R installation. You can download R freely from https://cran.r-project.org/ Follow the instruction to install it in your computer.

Though you can try most of the examples in R Console, I suggest you use RStudio. This IDE makes learning and using R easier. You can download RStudio from https://www.rstudio.com/. Follow the instruction to install it in your computer.

You will learn one-rule predictive modeling using the OneR package contributed by Holger K. von Jouanne-Diedrich.

Chapter 1: Building one-rule Model

This chapter covers the following topics:

- Data to predict
- OneR package and function
- Model fitting
- Predicting

The OneR function, provided by the OneR package, implements the one-rule algorithm. To build a predictive model we need to train the OneR function. We feed a training data to the OneR function. The function will learn from the data and build the model. This process is known as fitting the model to the data; the result is a fitted model.

The training data contains the result from past experiences, the results of credit card upgrade offers: Accepted or Declined.

Here's a sample of training data.

CARD	JOB	TRAVEL	MARITAL	UPGRADE
Gold	Admin	Rare	Married	Declined
Gold	Sales	Rare	Married	Declined
Silver	Admin	Frequent	Single	Accepted
Silver	Admin	Frequent	Married	Accepted
Gold	Sales	Occasiona	Divorced	Declined
Gold	Sales	Occasiona	Divorced	Declined
Silver	Sales	Occasiona	Divorced	Accepted
Gold	Sales	Frequent	Divorced	Accepted
Gold	Sales	Occasiona	Divorced	Declined
Gold	Admin	Frequent	Married	Accepted

Note that:

- The training data does not have the CARDHOLDER field, as we don't want to predict based on the cardholder names, we don't need it as a predictor.

- The UPGRADE column has values. We have the values, which are the results of the past upgrade offers. The algorithm needs to learn from these results.

Once you have the model, you can use the model to predict.

In the next sections you will learn the steps of training and predicting.

Installing OneR package

To try the book examples, you need to install the OneR package.

Your computer must have an internet connection. On the Console pane, at the command prompt >, type **install.packages("OneR")** and run it by pressing Ctrl + Enter.

```
install.packages("OneR")
```

```
## Warning in download.file(url, destfile, method, mode
= "wb", ...): cannot open
## URL 'http://anaconda-master.prodlb.travp.net/repo/re
pository/TrvRApprovedM/bin/
## windows/contrib/3.6/OneR_2.2.zip': HTTP status was '
404 bin/windows/contrib/3.6/
## OneR_2.2.zip'
```

```
## Error in download.file(url, destfile, method, mode =
"wb", ...) :
##    cannot open URL 'http://anaconda-master.prodlb.tra
vp.net/repo/repository/TrvRApprovedM/bin/windows/contri
b/3.6/OneR_2.2.zip'
```

```
## Warning in download.packages(pkgs, destdir = tmpd, a
vailable = available, :
## download of package 'OneR' failed
```

To test if the package is available for use, run the following command on the console. No error message means the package is available and ready for use.

```
library(OneR)
```

OneR function

The syntax of the function is as follows.

OneR(training_data, verbose = FALSE, ties.method = c("first", "chisq"))

tarining_data is a dataframe that contains the training data. The target column, UPGRADE, must be the last column; the other columns are treated as predictors.

If you set the verbose argument TRUE, you will get more information about the model. verbose default value is FALSE.

ties.method is used by the algorithm if two or more of the predictors have the same prediction accuracies.

We'll cover these two arguments a bit later.

Training a.k.a. Model Fitting

To build the model we will feed the training data to the OneR function.

Training data

Please prepare the following data, store it as ccuh.csv file. (ccuh stands for credit card upgrade history)

```
CARD,JOB,TRAVEL,MARITAL,UPGRADE
Gold,Admin,Rare,Married,Declined
Gold,Sales,Rare,Married,Declined
Silver,Admin,Frequent,Single,Accepted
Silver,Admin,Frequent,Married,Accepted
Gold,Sales,Occasional,Divorced,Declined
Gold,Sales,Occasional,Divorced,Declined
Silver,Sales,Occasional,Divorced,Accepted
Gold,Sales,Frequent,Divorced,Accepted
Gold,Sales,Occasional,Divorced,Declined
Gold,Admin,Frequent,Married,Accepted
```

Example 1.1 shows how to fit the OneR algorithm to the ccuh.csv training data.

The first command reads the training data from the csv file and stores the data in a variable named as a dataframe.
The second command loads the OneR package into the R workspace so that we can use the OneR function.
The third command calls the OneR function, passing the trd dataframe. The result, which is a one-rule model, is stored in ccuorm variable.
The last command, ccuorm, displays the model, the If - then rules. You will also see the accuracy of the model.

Example 1.1

```
# Load training data
trd <- read.csv("C:/OneR/ccuh.csv")
```

```
# fit model to trd 10 rows training data
library(OneR)
ccuorm <- OneR(trd)
ccuorm

##
## Call:
## OneR.data.frame(x = trd)
##
## Rules:
## If TRAVEL = Frequent   then UPGRADE = Accepted
## If TRAVEL = Occasional then UPGRADE = Declined
## If TRAVEL = Rare       then UPGRADE = Declined
##
## Accuracy:
## 9 of 10 instances classified correctly (90%)
```

Run the commands in Example 1.1, by pressing Ctrl + Alt + R,
you will see the model on the Console pane.

Predicting

Now that we can use the ccuorm model to predict.

Please create a sample data we want to predict as follows. Store the data in prd.csv file.

CARDHOLDER,CARD,JOB,TRAVEL,MARITAL
Andy,Gold,Admin,Frequent,Divorced
Dita,Silver,Sales,Frequent,Single
Anie,Silver,Sales,Occasional,Single
Istanto,Silver,Admin,Frequent,Single

Note that there's no target column, the UPGRADE.

To predict, use the predict() function from the OneR package.

The syntax of the function is:

predict(fitted_model, data_to_predict)

Prepare and run Example 1.2.

The predictions for the four cardholders are displayed where each column is the prediction of a cardholder.
The first cardholder, Ann, is a Frequent traveler hence the offer is predicted to be Accepted. The second, Dee, a Frequent traveler, Accepted; the third, an Occasional traveler, Declined; and lastly, the fourth, a Rare traveler, Declined.

Example 1.2

```
# load prd, data to predict
prd <- read.csv("C:/OneR/prd.csv")

# predict the upgrade offer to the cardholders in prd
predict(ccuorm, prd)

##    Frequent    Frequent Occasional       Rare
##    Accepted    Accepted   Declined   Declined
## Levels: Accepted Declined
```

UPGRADE prediction column

It would be nice to see the predictions, the resulting UPGRADE column, on the cardholders data being predicted.

The second last command in Example 1.3, prd$UPGRADE = pred adds the prediction result pred as the UPGRADE column to the prd data.

Prepare and run Example 1.3.

Example 1.3

```
# fit model to trd training data, 10 rows

library(OneR)
trd <- read.csv("C:/OneR/ccuh.csv")


ccuorm <- OneR(trd)
ccuorm

##
## Call:
## OneR.data.frame(x = trd)
##
## Rules:
## If TRAVEL = Frequent    then UPGRADE = Accepted
## If TRAVEL = Occasional then UPGRADE = Declined
## If TRAVEL = Rare        then UPGRADE = Declined
##
## Accuracy:
## 9 of 10 instances classified correctly (90%)

# data to predict
prd <- read.csv("C:/OneR/prd.csv")

# predict using the ccuorm model
prediction <- predict(ccuorm, prd, type = "class")

# Add prediction column UPGRADE to the prd.csv
prd$UPGRADE = prediction
prd
```

##	CARDHOLDER	CARD	JOB	TRAVEL	MARITAL	UPGRADEed
## 1	Ann	Gold	Admin	Frequent	Divorced	Accepted
## 2	Dee	Silver	Sales	Frequent	Single	Accepted
## 3	Alfonso	Silver	Sales	Occasional	Single	Declined
## 4	Isaac	Silver	Admin	Rare	Single	Declined

Chapter 2: Fitted model

This section of the book covers verbose argument of the OneR() function and the summary() function available in the OneR package.

- verbose argument for more model information.
- summary() function for more underlying information about the accuracy of the model.

verbose argument

Recall the syntax of the OneR function:

OneR(dataframe, verbose = FALSE, ties.method = c("first", "chisq"))

So far, our examples took the default FALSE of the verbose argument.

With verbose = FALSE, when you invoke the OneR() function, no output is displayed. Example 2.1 uses the default verbose = FALSE.

Example 2.1: verbose = FALSE

```
# load training data
trd <- read.csv("C:/OneR/ccuh.csv")

# fit model to trd 10 rows training data
library(OneR)
ccuorm <- OneR(trd)
ccuorm

##
## Call:
## OneR.data.frame(x = trd)
##
## Rules:
## If TRAVEL = Frequent   then UPGRADE = Accepted
## If TRAVEL = Occasional then UPGRADE = Declined
## If TRAVEL = Rare       then UPGRADE = Declined
```

```
##
## Accuracy:
## 9 of 10 instances classified correctly (90%)
```

If you set the verbose argument to TRUE, the list of predictors with their accuracies are displayed, and the chosen predictor is marked with *.

Prepare and run Example 2.2.
You will see the predictor accuracy ranking. comparing the outputs of the 1st call to the 2nd, you can see the 2nd with verbose = TRUE has the accuracy ranking of the predictors.

Example 2.2: verbose = TRUE

```
# load training data
trd <- read.csv("C:/OneR/ccuh.csv")

# fit model to trd 10 rows training data
library(OneR)

# verbose = TRUE to display attributes accuracy ranking
OneR(trd, verbose = TRUE)

##
##      Attribute Accuracy
## 1 * TRAVEL     90%
## 2   CARD       80%
## 3   JOB        70%
## 4   MARITAL    60%
## ---
## Chosen attribute due to accuracy
## and ties method (if applicable): '*'

##
## Call:
## OneR.data.frame(x = trd, verbose = TRUE)
##
## Rules:
## If TRAVEL = Frequent   then UPGRADE = Accepted
## If TRAVEL = Occasional then UPGRADE = Declined
## If TRAVEL = Rare       then UPGRADE = Declined
```

```
##
## Accuracy:
## 9 of 10 instances classified correctly (90%)
```

summary function

A summary() function is available in the OneR package. The function displays two additional information about the model: Contingency table of the selected predictor and chi-squared test result.

The last command in Example 2.3 invoke the summary() function, the contigency table and p-value are displayed.

Example 2.3: summary function

```
# load training data
trd <- read.csv("C:/OneR/ccuh.csv")

# fit model to trd 10 rows training data
library(OneR)
ccuorm <- OneR(trd)

summary(ccuorm) # displays Contingency table of the sel
ected predictor and the result of chi-squared test

##
## Call:
## OneR.data.frame(x = trd)
##
## Rules:
## If TRAVEL = Frequent    then UPGRADE = Accepted
## If TRAVEL = Occasional  then UPGRADE = Declined
## If TRAVEL = Rare        then UPGRADE = Declined
##
## Accuracy:
## 9 of 10 instances classified correctly (90%)
##
## Contingency table:
##             TRAVEL
## UPGRADE     Frequent Occasional Rare Sum
##    Accepted     * 4           1    0   5
##    Declined       0         * 3  * 2   5
##    Sum            4           4    2  10
## ---
## Maximum in each column: '*'
```

```
##
## Pearson's Chi-squared test:
## X-squared = 7, df = 2, p-value = 0.0302
```

Content of the OneR Model

The oneR model created (the fitted model) is a list as confirmed by is.list(ccuorm) in Example 2.4.

The str(ccuorm) displays the elements of the ccuorm list. The list has 7 elements (list of 7). You can see the names of the elements: **call** (on the call to OneR function we passed the data.frame argument), **target** (target variable), **feature** (predictor variable), and so on.

Example 2.4: fitted model is a list

```
is.list(ccuorm)

## [1] TRUE

str(ccuorm)

## List of 7
##  $ call              : language OneR.data.frame(x = t
rd)
##  $ target            : chr "UPGRADE"
##  $ feature           : chr "TRAVEL"
##  $ rules             :List of 3
##   ..$ Frequent  : chr "Accepted"
##   ..$ Occasional: chr "Declined"
##   ..$ Rare      : chr "Declined"
##  $ correct_instances: num 9
##  $ total_instances  : int 10
##  $ cont_table       : 'table' int [1:2, 1:3] 4 0 1 3
0 2
##   ..- attr(*, "dimnames")=List of 2
##   .. ..$ UPGRADE: chr [1:2] "Accepted" "Declined"
##   .. ..$ TRAVEL : chr [1:3] "Frequent" "Occasional"
"Rare"
##  - attr(*, "class")= chr "OneR"
```

Plotting

The OneR package provides a plot() function to visualize the contingency table of the model.

Try Example 2.5

Accepted is dark plotted, Declined is clear.

- All (four) Frequent is Accepted - Frequent is all dark plotted
- One Occasional is Accepted; three, Declined - one fourth is dark, three fourth are clear
- All two Rare's are Declined - all is clear

Example 2.5: Plot of contingency table

```
# load training data
trd <- read.csv("C:/OneR/ccuh.csv")

# fit model to trd 10 rows training data
library(OneR)
ccuorm <- OneR(trd) # verbose = TRUE display the predic
tors ranking
summary(ccuorm)

##
## Call:
## OneR.data.frame(x = trd)
##
## Rules:
## If TRAVEL = Frequent   then UPGRADE = Accepted
## If TRAVEL = Occasional then UPGRADE = Declined
## If TRAVEL = Rare       then UPGRADE = Declined
##
## Accuracy:
## 9 of 10 instances classified correctly (90%)
##
## Contingency table:
##               TRAVEL
## UPGRADE    Frequent Occasional Rare Sum
##    Accepted     * 4          1    0   5
##    Declined       0        * 3  * 2   5
```

```
##    Sum                    4              4    2   10
## ---
## Maximum in each column: '*'
##
## Pearson's Chi-squared test:
## X-squared = 7, df = 2, p-value = 0.0302
```

```
plot(ccuorm)
```

OneR model diagnostic plot

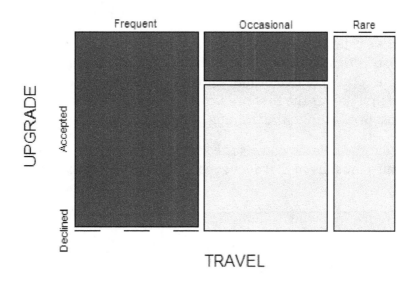

Chapter 3: ties.methods argument

Recall that the syntax of the OneR function is:

OneR(**dataframe**, verbose = FALSE, ties.method = c("first", "chisq"))

When the function finds two or more most accurate predictors with the same accuracy, the ties.method value determines the selection of the of predictor column for the model.

default ties.method = c("first", "chisq")

So far, we called the function with the default verbose = **c("chisq", "first")** This default argument means, if there's a tie (same accuracy) of two or more predictor, first is performed, where first means the first predictor in the sequence, or the leftmost predictor, in the training data is selected.

Note that the default value is precisely c("first", "chisq"), the first and chisq must be in that sequence, c("chisq", "first") is not the same.

Prepare the following training data.

CARD,WORK,MARITAL,TRAVEL,UPGRADE
Silver,Sales,Divorced,Rare,Declined
Silver,Sales,Divorced,Rare,Declined
Gold,Admin,Single,Frequent,Accepted
Gold,Admin,Single,Frequent,Accepted
Silver,Sales,Marriedd,Occasional,Declined
Silver,Sales,Marriedd,Occasional,Declined

In Example 3.1 all four predictors have the same accuracy, 100%, hence the first predictor, CARD, is selected.

Example 3.1: CARD is first column

```
library(OneR)
trdsa <- read.csv("C:/OneR/ccsa.csv") # trdsa stands fo
```

r training data, same accuracies
```
ccuorm <- OneR(trdsa, verbose = TRUE)

##
##         Attribute Accuracy
## 1 *  CARD        100%
## 1     WORK        100%
## 1     MARITAL     100%
## 1     TRAVEL      100%
## ---
## Chosen attribute due to accuracy
## and ties method (if applicable): '*'

summary(ccuorm)

##
## Call:
## OneR.data.frame(x = trdsa, verbose = TRUE)
##
## Rules:
## If CARD = Gold   then UPGRADE = Accepted
## If CARD = Silver then UPGRADE = Declined
##
## Accuracy:
## 6 of 6 instances classified correctly (100%)
##
## Contingency table:
##            CARD
## UPGRADE     Gold Silver Sum
##    Accepted * 2      0    2
##    Declined   0    * 4    4
##    Sum        2      4    6
## ---
## Maximum in each column: '*'
##
## Pearson's Chi-squared test:
## X-squared = 2.3438, df = 1, p-value = 0.1258
```

In Example 3.2, the **trdsa[, c(2,1,3,4,5)]** command switches the first two columns, WORK is now the first column, hence it is selected.

Example 3.2: MARITAL is first column

```
library(OneR)
trdsa <- read.csv("C:/OneR/ccsa.csv")
trdsa <- trdsa[, c(2,1,3,4,5)]
trdsa
```

```
##     WORK   CARD  MARITAL      TRAVEL  UPGRADE
## 1 Sales Silver Divorced        Rare Declined
## 2 Sales Silver Divorced        Rare Declined
## 3 Admin   Gold   Single    Frequent Accepted
## 4 Admin   Gold   Single    Frequent Accepted
## 5 Sales Silver Marriedd Occasional Declined
## 6 Sales Silver Marriedd Occasional Declined
```

```
ccuorm <- OneR(trdsa, verbose = TRUE)
```

```
##
##        Attribute Accuracy
## 1 * WORK         100%
## 1   CARD         100%
## 1   MARITAL      100%
## 1   TRAVEL       100%
## ---
## Chosen attribute due to accuracy
## and ties method (if applicable): '*'
```

```
summary(ccuorm)
```

```
##
## Call:
## OneR.data.frame(x = trdsa, verbose = TRUE)
##
## Rules:
## If WORK = Admin then UPGRADE = Accepted
## If WORK = Sales then UPGRADE = Declined
##
## Accuracy:
## 6 of 6 instances classified correctly (100%)
##
## Contingency table:
##              WORK
## UPGRADE    Admin Sales Sum
```

```
##     Accepted  * 2     0    2
##     Declined    0   * 4    4
##     Sum         2     4    6
## ---
## Maximum in each column: '*'
##
## Pearson's Chi-squared test:
## X-squared = 2.3438, df = 1, p-value = 0.1258
```

Let's next learn the ties.method = "chisq".

ties.method = chisq

If ties.method = "chisq" and we have two or more tied columns, the column with the lowest p-value of the chi-squared test is selected.

Example 3.3 applies chisq. Notice that p-value of MARITAL is 0.04979. If you look back at Example 3.1 and 3.2, the p-value of both CARD and WORK is 0.1258, which is higher than that of MARITAL. We'll see in Example 3.4 that the p-value of TRAVEL is also 0.04979. But MARITAL is earlier (first) in the sequence than TRAVEL, hence TRAVEL is selected.

Example 3.3: chisq

```
library(OneR)
trdsa <- read.csv("C:/OneR/ccsa.csv")
ccuorm <- OneR(trdsa, verbose = TRUE, ties.method = "ch
isq")

##
##      Attribute Accuracy
## 1    CARD       100%
## 1    WORK       100%
## 1 * MARITAL     100%
## 1    TRAVEL     100%
## ---
## Chosen attribute due to accuracy
## and ties method (if applicable): '*'

summary(ccuorm)

##
## Call:
## OneR.data.frame(x = trdsa, ties.method = "chisq", ve
rbose = TRUE)
##
## Rules:
## If MARITAL = Divorced then UPGRADE = Declined
## If MARITAL = Marriedd then UPGRADE = Declined
```

```
## If MARITAL = Single    then UPGRADE = Accepted
##
## Accuracy:
## 6 of 6 instances classified correctly (100%)
##
## Contingency table:
##              MARITAL
## UPGRADE    Divorced  Married Single Sum
##    Accepted        0        0   * 2   2
##    Declined      * 2      * 2     0   4
##    Sum             2        2     2   6
## ---
## Maximum in each column: '*'
##
## Pearson's Chi-squared test:
## X-squared = 6, df = 2, p-value = 0.04979
```

In Example 3.4 we switch the sequence of MARITAL and TRAVEL, TRAVEL is now ahead of MARITAL. You can see that TRAVEL's p-value is also 0.04979, which the same as MARITAL's that you saw in Example 3.3. Hence, TRAVEL is selected.

Example 3.4: chisq

```
library(OneR)
trdsa <- read.csv("C:/OneR/ccsa.csv")
trdsa <- trdsa[, c(1,2,4,3,5)]
ccuorm <- OneR(trdsa, verbose = TRUE, ties.method = "ch
isq")

##
##       Attribute Accuracy
## 1     CARD      100%
## 1     WORK      100%
## 1 *   TRAVEL    100%
## 1     MARITAL   100%
## ---
## Chosen attribute due to accuracy
## and ties method (if applicable): '*'

summary(ccuorm)
```

```
##
## Call:
## OneR.data.frame(x = trdsa, ties.method = "chisq", ve
rbose = TRUE)
##
## Rules:
## If TRAVEL = Frequent   then UPGRADE = Accepted
## If TRAVEL = Occasional then UPGRADE = Declined
## If TRAVEL = Rare       then UPGRADE = Declined
##
## Accuracy:
## 6 of 6 instances classified correctly (100%)
##
## Contingency table:
##             TRAVEL
## UPGRADE    Frequent Occasional Rare Sum
##   Accepted      * 2          0    0   2
##   Declined        0        * 2  * 2   4
##   Sum             2          2    2   6
## ---
## Maximum in each column: '*'
##
## Pearson's Chi-squared test:
## X-squared = 6, df = 2, p-value = 0.04979
```

ties.method = first

ties.method = "first" works the same as that of the default
ties.method = c("first", "chisq")

If you run Example 3.5 and 3.6 below, the resulting model should
be the same that of Example 3.1 and 3.2 above.

Example 3.5: CARD is first column

```
library(OneR)
trdsa <- read.csv("C:/OneR/ccsa.csv") # trdsa stands fo
r training data, same accuracies
ccuorm <- OneR(trdsa, verbose = TRUE, ties.method = "fi
rst")
```

```
##
##      Attribute Accuracy
## 1 * CARD       100%
## 1   WORK       100%
## 1   MARITAL    100%
## 1   TRAVEL     100%
## ---
## Chosen attribute due to accuracy
## and ties method (if applicable): '*'
```

```
summary(ccuorm)
```

```
##
## Call:
## OneR.data.frame(x = trdsa, ties.method = "first", ve
rbose = TRUE)
##
## Rules:
## If CARD = Gold   then UPGRADE = Accepted
## If CARD = Silver then UPGRADE = Declined
##
## Accuracy:
## 6 of 6 instances classified correctly (100%)
##
## Contingency table:
##             CARD
## UPGRADE     Gold Silver Sum
##    Accepted * 2       0   2
##    Declined   0     * 4   4
##    Sum        2       4   6
## ---
## Maximum in each column: '*'
##
## Pearson's Chi-squared test:
## X-squared = 2.3438, df = 1, p-value = 0.1258
```

Example 3.6: MARITAL is first column

```
library(OneR)
trdsa <- read.csv("C:/OneR/ccsa.csv")
trdsa <- trdsa[, c(2,1,3,4,5)]
trdsa
```

```
##     WORK   CARD  MARITAL     TRAVEL  UPGRADE
## 1 Sales Silver Divorced       Rare Declined
## 2 Sales Silver Divorced       Rare Declined
## 3 Admin   Gold   Single   Frequent Accepted
## 4 Admin   Gold   Single   Frequent Accepted
## 5 Sales Silver Marriedd Occasional Declined
## 6 Sales Silver Marriedd Occasional Declined
```

```
ccuorm <- OneR(trdsa, verbose = TRUE, ties.method = "fi
rst")
```

```
##
##      Attribute Accuracy
## 1 * WORK       100%
## 1   CARD       100%
## 1   MARITAL    100%
## 1   TRAVEL     100%
## ---
## Chosen attribute due to accuracy
## and ties method (if applicable): '*'
```

```
summary(ccuorm)
```

```
##
## Call:
## OneR.data.frame(x = trdsa, ties.method = "first", ve
rbose = TRUE)
##
## Rules:
## If WORK = Admin then UPGRADE = Accepted
## If WORK = Sales then UPGRADE = Declined
##
## Accuracy:
## 6 of 6 instances classified correctly (100%)
##
## Contingency table:
##           WORK
## UPGRADE    Admin Sales Sum
##   Accepted * 2      0   2
##   Declined   0    * 4   4
##   Sum        2      4   6
## ---
```

```
## Maximum in each column: '*'
##
## Pearson's Chi-squared test:
## X-squared = 2.3438, df = 1, p-value = 0.1258
```

Chapter 4: Numeric data

So far, all columns are non-numeric. Both predictor and target can be numeric.

Numeric Predictor

The OneR function converts numeric predictor column into five bins of equal length if the column has more than five distinct values.

Assume we have the following training data.

Age,Income,Upgrade
25,60000,No
30,60000,Yes
35,90000,Yes
40,95000,Yes
50,100000,Yes
60,100000,No

As we have six distinct ages, the OneR() will convert them into five categories.

Prepare and run Example 4.1. You will see the factor of five levels under the Rules. The Contingency table also shows the five categories.

Example 4.1

```
library(OneR)
ccd <- read.csv("C:/OneR/age6.csv") # num6 stands for s
ix data with 6 distinc ages
print(ccd)
```

```
##    Age Income Upgrade
## 1  25  60000      No
## 2  30  60000     Yes
## 3  35  90000     Yes
## 4  40  95000     Yes
## 5  50 100000     Yes
## 6  60 100000      No
```

```
ccuorm <- OneR(ccd, verbose = TRUE)
```

```
##
##       Attribute Accuracy
## 1 *  Age        83.33%
## 2    Income     66.67%
## ---
## Chosen attribute due to accuracy
## and ties method (if applicable): '*'
```

```
summary(ccuorm)
```

```
##
## Call:
## OneR.data.frame(x = ccd, verbose = TRUE)
##
## Rules:
## If Age = (25,32] then Upgrade = No
## If Age = (32,39] then Upgrade = Yes
## If Age = (39,46] then Upgrade = Yes
## If Age = (46,53] then Upgrade = Yes
## If Age = (53,60] then Upgrade = No
##
## Accuracy:
## 5 of 6 instances classified correctly (83.33%)
##
## Contingency table:
##         Age
## Upgrade (25,32] (32,39] (39,46] (46,53] (53,60] Sum
##    No     * 1       0       0       0     * 1    2
##    Yes      1     * 1     * 1     * 1       0    4
##    Sum      2       1       1       1       1    6
## ---
## Maximum in each column: '*'
```

```
##
## Pearson's Chi-squared test:
## X-squared = 3.75, df = 4, p-value = 0.4409
```

If age has five or less distinct values, they will not be converted into five categories, they will be used as-is.

Run Example 4.2 with the following age5.csv training data, which has five distinct ages.

Age,Income,Upgrade
25,60000,No
30,60000,Yes
35,90000,Yes
40,95000,Yes
50,100000,Yes
50,100000,No
40,60000,No

Example 4.2

```
library(OneR)
ccd <- read.csv("C:/OneR/age5.csv") # num6 stands for s
ix data with 5 distinc ages
print(ccd)

##    Age Income Upgrade
## 1   25  60000      No
## 2   30  60000     Yes
## 3   35  90000     Yes
## 4   40  95000     Yes
## 5   50 100000     Yes
## 6   50 100000      No

ccuorm <- OneR(ccd, verbose = TRUE)

##
##        Attribute Accuracy
## 1 *   Age         83.33%
## 2     Income      66.67%
## ---
```

```
## Chosen attribute due to accuracy
## and ties method (if applicable): '*'

summary(ccuorm)

##
## Call:
## OneR.data.frame(x = ccd, verbose = TRUE)
##
## Rules:
## If Age = 25 then Upgrade = No
## If Age = 30 then Upgrade = Yes
## If Age = 35 then Upgrade = Yes
## If Age = 40 then Upgrade = Yes
## If Age = 50 then Upgrade = No
##
## Accuracy:
## 5 of 6 instances classified correctly (83.33%)
##
## Contingency table:
##           Age
## Upgrade   25   30   35   40   50 Sum
##     No  * 1    0    0    0  * 1   2
##     Yes   0  * 1  * 1  * 1    1   4
##     Sum   1    1    1    1    2   6
## ---
## Maximum in each column: '*'
##
## Pearson's Chi-squared test:
## X-squared = 3.75, df = 4, p-value = 0.4409
```

Numeric Target

We will use the following training data, target.csv, where the target is SPENDING, a numeric target. SPENDING has eight levels: 40, 45, 50, 55, 60, 65. 70 and 75. The selected predictor is AGE, happens to be numeric with eight levels as well. Hence, they are both converted to five categories.

RESIDENT,GENDER,AGE,SPENDING
Own,Male,25,40,No

```
Rent,Male,30,45,Yes
Rent,Male,35,50,Yes
Rent,Male,40,55,Yes
Own,Female,45,60,Yes
Own,Female,60,65,No
Own,Male,65,75,No
Rent,Female,65,55,No
Own,Male,65,65,No
Rent,Female,70,40,No
Rent,Female,70,50,No
Rent,Female,70,70,No
```

Example 4.3

```
library(OneR)
ccd <- read.csv("C:/OneR/target.csv")
ccd

##       RESIDENT GENDER AGE SPENDING
## 1          Own   Male  25       40
## 2         Rent   Male  30       45
## 3         Rent   Male  35       50
## 4         Rent   Male  40       55
## 5          Own Female  45       60
## 6          Own Female  60       65
## 7          Own   Male  65       75
## 8         Rent Female  65       55
## 9          Own   Male  65       65
## 10        Rent Female  70       40
## 11        Rent Female  70       50
## 12        Rent Female  70       70

ccuorm <- OneR(ccd, verbose = TRUE)

##
##       Attribute Accuracy
## 1 * AGE         58.33%
## 2   RESIDENT    33.33%
## 2   GENDER      33.33%
## ---
## Chosen attribute due to accuracy
## and ties method (if applicable): '*'
```

```
summary(ccuorm)

##
## Call:
## OneR.data.frame(x = ccd, verbose = TRUE)
##
## Rules:
## If AGE = (25,34] then SPENDING = (40,47]
## If AGE = (34,43] then SPENDING = (47,54]
## If AGE = (43,52] then SPENDING = (54,61]
## If AGE = (52,61] then SPENDING = (61,68]
## If AGE = (61,70] then SPENDING = (68,75]
##
## Accuracy:
## 7 of 12 instances classified correctly (58.33%)
##
## Contingency table:
##              AGE
## SPENDING  (25,34] (34,43] (43,52] (52,61] (61,70] Su
m
##    (40,47]     * 2       0       0       0       1
3
##    (47,54]       0     * 1       0       0       1
2
##    (54,61]       0       1     * 1       0       1
3
##    (61,68]       0       0       0     * 1       1
2
##    (68,75]       0       0       0       0     * 2
2
##    Sum           2       2       1       1       6 1
2
## ---
## Maximum in each column: '*'
##
## Pearson's Chi-squared test:
## X-squared = 18.333, df = 16, p-value = 0.3047
```

Chapter 5: UNSEEN predictor

If the data to be predicted is not in the model, then it will be predicted as UNSEEN.

Prepare the following data to try Example 5.1
The last row has **Seldom** on the TRAVEL predictor. As Seldom not in the model, its UPGRADE prediction is UNSEEN.

TRAVEL,MARITAL,WORK,CARD
Rare,Single,Sales,Silver
Rare,Kids,Office,Gold
Frequent,Kids,Office,Silver
Occasional,Single,Sales,Silver
Occasional,Couple,Office,Gold
Seldom,Couple,Sales,Bronze

Example 5.1

```
# load training data
trd <- read.csv("C:/OneR/ccuh.csv")

# fit model to trd 10 rows training data
library(OneR)
ccuorm <- OneR(trd)

# predict unseen
prd_unseen <- read.csv("C:/OneR/unseen.csv")
prd_unseen
```

```
##            TRAVEL MARITAL   WORK    CARD
## 1            Rare  Single  Sales  Silver
## 2            Rare    Kids Office    Gold
## 3        Frequent    Kids Office  Silver
## 4 Occasional    Single  Sales  Silver
## 5 Occasional  Couple Office    Gold
## 6          Seldom  Couple  Sales  Bronce
```

```
predict(ccuorm, prd_unseen)
```

```
##          Rare        Rare  Frequent Occasional Occasion
## al      Seldom
```

```
##    Declined    Declined    Accepted    Declined    Declin
ed        UNSEEN
## Levels: Accepted Declined UNSEEN
```

Chapter 6: OneR() Function with Formula

You learned in the previous chapter that the One() function with dataframe requires the target variable as the last column.

What if the target column of your dataframe is not the last column and/or you want only some of the other columns as predictors?

The OneR() with **formula** flavor comes handy to cope with these needs.

The syntax is as follows.

OneR(**formula, data**, ties.method = c("first", "chisq"), verbose = FALSE)

formula is an expression in the form:

target_column ~ predictor_column1 + predictor_column2 + ...

In Example 6.1 the credit_card_formula.csv the target variable Upgrade is not the last column.

CARD,JOB,UPGRADE,TRAVEL,MARITAL
Gold,Admin,Declined,Rare,Married
Gold,Sales,Declined,Rare,Married
Silver,Admin,Accepted,Frequent,Single
Silver,Admin,Accepted,Frequent,Married
Gold,Sales,Declined,Occasional,Divorced
Gold,Sales,Declined,Occasional,Divorced
Silver,Sales,Accepted,Occasional,Divorced
Gold,Sales,Accepted,Frequent,Divorced
Gold,Sales,Declined,Occasional,Divorced
Gold,Admin,Accepted,Frequent,Married

In Example 6.1 we specify only three predictor variables.

To try Example 6.1, you need to prepare the
credit_card_formula.csv.

Example 6.1

```
library(OneR)
ccd <- read.csv("ccuf.csv")
ccuorm <- OneR(UPGRADE ~ JOB + MARITAL, ccd, verbose =
TRUE)

##
##       Attribute Accuracy
## 1 * JOB          70%
## 2    MARITAL     60%
## ---
## Chosen attribute due to accuracy
## and ties method (if applicable): '*'

summary(ccuorm)

##
## Call:
## OneR.formula(formula = UPGRADE ~ JOB + MARITAL, data
= ccd, verbose = TRUE)
##
## Rules:
## If JOB = Admin then UPGRADE = Accepted
## If JOB = Sales then UPGRADE = Declined
##
## Accuracy:
## 7 of 10 instances classified correctly (70%)
##
## Contingency table:
##            JOB
## UPGRADE    Admin Sales Sum
##   Accepted  * 3    2    5
##   Declined    1  * 4    5
##   Sum         4    6   10
## ---
## Maximum in each column: '*'
##
```

```
## Pearson's Chi-squared test:
## X-squared = 0.41667, df = 1, p-value = 0.5186
```

Appendix: R Tutorials for Beginners

In R, a computation (data processing) happens by calling (invoking) a function call. The function operates on the objects supplied (passed) as its arguments. That's it, function and object.

in this appendix, you will learn how to interact with R, use some of commonly used functions and objects.

Command, Script and Comment

You interact with R by executing commands.

Example A.1 is one line script, the print("Hello, World!") is a command to display the "Hello, World!" greeting on the console.

Example A.1

```
print("Hello, World!")

## [1] "Hello, World!"
```

You will use RSutdio to try the exammples.

- Start your RStudio.
- Type the Example A.1 on your Script pane.
- While your cursor is still on the line, press Ctrl + Enter. You can also press Ctrl + Alt + r, regardless the location of your cursor, which will execute all lines, the whole script.

The command is seen executed on the Console and the greeting is displayed.

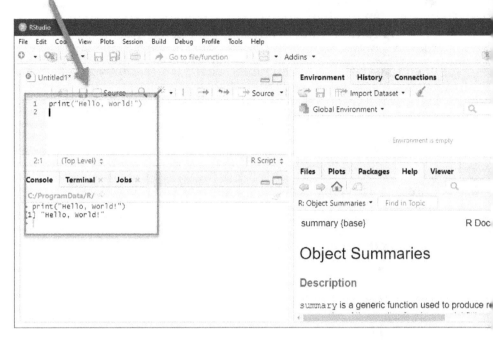

If your Console gets cluttered, you can clear it by pressing Ctrl + l.

You can save your script by pressing **Ctrl + s**. You can open the script back in the script pane from a file by pressing **Ctrl + o** and select the file. In a real development project, where you will have many lines in the script, you will want to save your working script regularly. In case something unexpected happens, you have a recent backup of your script that you can reload into RStudio.

Anything on a line after a # is a comment. Comments are not executable command, they serve as notes, inline documentation in the script.

The script in Example A.2 has two comments.

Example A.2

```r
# To get iniated into R
print("Welcome to the Exciting World of R!")  # print (
display) the R greeting
```

```
## [1] "Welcome to the Exciting World of R!"
```

The whole line 1 is a comment. Excute line 1 by placing your cursor on the line and press **Ctrl+Enter**. Nothing happens as expected.

Line 2 has # but not at the beginning of the line. The command before the #, print("Welcome to the Exciting World of R!"), is executed, while the comment **# print (display) the R greeting** will not.

Please try Example A.2.

R ignores white spaces. In Example A.3 the two print commands, though the second has noticeably extra white spaces, produce the same result as Example A.2.

Example A.3

```
print("When you finish reading the book, you'd like R e
ven more!")
```

```
## [1] "When you finish reading the book, you'd like R
even more!"
```

```
print (      "When you finish reading the book, you'd li
ke R even more!"      )
```

```
## [1] "When you finish reading the book, you'd like R
even more!"
```

You can execute the two commands by selecting them and press Ctrl + Enter.

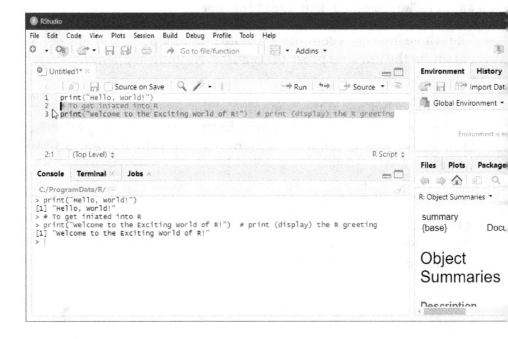

Package, Function and Data

Function and data lie at the heart of R. Related functions and data are usually put together into a package.

Note that technically, data is an object, a type of object in R. Function is also an object, a different object type from data. If you want to explore more about objects visit https://cran.r-project.org/doc/manuals/r-release/R-lang.html

Package

In R, we usually put together related functions, data and documentation in a package.

To use a function from a package, you must have installed the package in your computer. Some packages are included in the R installation, such as **base**, **stats**, **datasets**, and **grDevices**.

To install a package on your computer, run the install.packages("packagename") command.

In this book, we use OneR package. If you have not installed it, after making sure your computer has an internet connection, on the Console pane, at the command prompt >, type **install.packages("OneR")** and run it by pressing Ctrl + Enter.

To see the content of a package, issue an ls("package:name") command. ls("package:OneR") will show you the list of the content of the OneR package.

When you try Example A.4 you will see that the OneR package has one dataset, "breastcancer", and six functions, one of which **OneR** we use in this book for creating one-role predictive model.

Example A.4

```
library(OneR)
ls("package:OneR")
```

```
## [1] "bin"          "breastcancer" "eval_model"  "is
.OneR"      "maxlevels"
## [6] "OneR"         "optbin"
```

Function

In Example A.4. the **library()**, read.csv() and **print()** are functions readily available; while the OneR() function is available only when you have installed the OneR package. In this book, I mention a function by its name followed by empty parantheses like those in the previous sentence.

Once a package is installed, you can use the functions from the package. The second command in Example A.5 shows how to use the OneR function from the OneR package. The syntax is **package::function()**.

To try Example A.5 you need to create a ccuh.csv file that contains the following records:

CARD,JOB,TRAVEL,MARITAL,UPGRADE
Gold,Admin,Rare,Married,Declined
Gold,Sales,Rare,Married,Declined
Silver,Admin,Frequent,Single,Accepted
Silver,Admin,Frequent,Married,Accepted
Gold,Sales,Occasional,Divorced,Declined
Gold,Sales,Occasional,Divorced,Declined
Silver,Sales,Occasional,Divorced,Accepted
Gold,Sales,Frequent,Divorced,Accepted
Gold,Sales,Occasional,Divorced,Declined
Gold,Admin,Frequent,Married,Accepted

The first line invokes read.csv() function to read the ccuh.csv file and stores the data in a variable named ccd. The second line invokes OneR() function passing the ccd data as its argument to create a one-rule model, the resulting model is stored in a variable named ccuorm.
The third line display the model.

You can learn the details of the OneR() function in the main part of the books: Chapter 1 to 6.

Example A.5

```
library(OneR)
setwd("C:/OneR/")
ccd <- read.csv("ccuh.csv")
ccuorm <- OneR::OneR(ccd)
ccuorm

##
## Call:
## OneR.data.frame(x = ccd)
##
## Rules:
## If TRAVEL = Frequent   then UPGRADE = Accepted
## If TRAVEL = Occasional then UPGRADE = Declined
## If TRAVEL = Rare       then UPGRADE = Declined
##
## Accuracy:
## 9 of 10 instances classified correctly (90%)
```

When you execute the lines in Example A.5, you will see the objects listed on the top right-hand corner, the Environment pane.

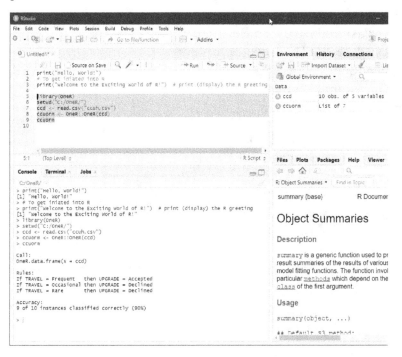

If you will use a function more than just once or use more than just one function from a package, you would better load the package. The syntax of the command to load a package is library(packagename). You can then use in your script any of the objects without specifying the package name. Example A.6 shows the use of library().

Example A.6

```
library(OneR)
ccuhd <- read.csv("C:/OneR/ccuh.csv")
ccuorm <- OneR(ccuhd)
print(ccuorm)

##
## Call:
## OneR.data.frame(x = ccuhd)
##
## Rules:
## If TRAVEL = Frequent    then UPGRADE = Accepted
## If TRAVEL = Occasional then UPGRADE = Declined
## If TRAVEL = Rare        then UPGRADE = Declined
##
## Accuracy:
## 9 of 10 instances classified correctly (90%)
```

Arguments

Function can have one or more arguments. When you call (use) a function and the function expects one or more arguments, you should pass (provide) them. Arguments are provided in parentheses after the function name.

In the three functions in Example A.6, we pass one argument to the three function: library(), read.csv() and OneR().

In Example A.7 below the paste() has five arguments separated by a comma. The first three arguments are three strings to be pasted together, the fourth is a calculation, and the fifth is the separator of between the three strings. For the sep argument we want ... as the separator.

Example A.7

```
paste("The result of calculating", "1 * 2 / 100", "is",
1*2/100, sep = ' ... ')

## [1] "The result of calculating ... 1 * 2 / 100 ... i
s ... 0.02"
```

When we call a function and pass its arguments, we can provide the name of the argument.

Let's look at the syntax of the paste() function.

paste(object1, object2, ..., sep = " ")

Default of Argument

sep = " " means the default value of the sep argument is a space, i.e. if you call the paste() function without the sep argument, the separator will be a space.

Example A.8

```
paste("The result of calculating", "1 * 2 / 100", "is",
1*2/100)

## [1] "The result of calculating 1 * 2 / 100 is 0.02"
```

The first two calls to the paste() function in Example A.9 pass the sep arguments. The difference between the first and the second call is the positions of the sep argument, but the result is the same, meaning as long as you specify the name, i.e. **sep**, regardless where you specify it relative to the other arguments, the sep argument effect is the same.

Example A.9

```
paste("object1", "object2", sep=" > > > ")

## [1] "object1 > > > object2"

paste("object1", sep=" > > > ", "object2")

## [1] "object1 > > > object2"
```

Argument by position and name

The seq.int() function has the following syntax.

seq.int(from, to, by)

Notice the positions of the arguments: from is the first; to the second; and, by the third.

In Example A.10, the first call supplies the three arguments by their positions as specified in the syntax: the 10 is for the **from** argument; 20 for the **to** argument; and, 2 for the **by** argument.

If you want to supply the arguments not by the positions as in the syntax, use the names of the arguments; the second call to the seq.int() is an example.

Example A.10

```
seq.int(10, 20, 2)

## [1] 10 12 14 16 18 20

seq.int(to = 50, by = 5, from = 25)

## [1] 25 30 35 40 45 50
```

Help on Function

To find out more about a function, use help. When you execute the command in Example 3.4, you will see the information about the function displayed on the Help pane.

Example A.11

```
help(paste)

## starting httpd help server ... done
```

The information is for example about the arguments. In addition to the character strings to be concatenated together as arguments, you can also specify the separation string on the **sep** argument. In Example A.12 the separator is =.

Example A.12

```
stringargs <- paste("The result of calculating", "1 * 2
/ 100")
paste(stringargs, 1 + 2 / 100, sep = " = ")

## [1] "The result of calculating 1 * 2 / 100 = 1.02"
```

Function Nesting

Function can be nested, meaning you pass a function call as an argument of its parent function call.

In Example A.13 we nest sqrt() function under cumsum() function and c() function under sqrt() function, a three level nesting.

The c(4, 16) produces two numbers, 4 and 6, which the sqrt() function takes the square root of each, producing 2 and 3. The outermost function, cum() produces the ultimate output of the command, the cumulative sum of the 2 that is 2, and the cumulative sum of 2 and 3 that is 5.

Try Example A.13. Do you get the result as expected?

Example A.13

```
cumsum(sqrt(c(4, 9)))

## [1] 2 5
```

Vector

In R, data is stored in data structure. Vector is one of the data structures.

Let's take a look at Example A.14.

In the command **hw <- c("Hello, World!")**, the function **c("Hello, World!")** creates a vector with one element, the "Hello, World!" data.

The **assignment operator <-** assigns the vector to a object named **hw**. We can then refer to the vector as hw.

The second command, **print(hw)** displays the data in the hw vector, "Hello, World!", on the Console.

Some commands, such as the hw <- c("Hello, World!"), do not result in displayable output.

"Hello, World!" is a character string, hence the hw data type is character, we say, hw is character vector.

The call to typeof function, the typeof(hw) in Example 3.8 checks the type of the hw vector. When you run the script you will see the command output confirms that hw is indeed a **character** vector.

Example A.14

```
hw <- c("Hello, World!")
print(hw)

## [1] "Hello, World!"

typeof(hw)

## [1] "character"
```

Logical Vector

Elements of a logical element can only be TRUE or FALSE. T and F are equivalent to TRUE and FALSE, respectively.

A logical vector, lgl, is created in Example A.15.

The typeof(lgl) proves that lgl is indeed a logical vector.

The five elements are displayed by the print(lgl)

Example A.15

```
lgl <- c(TRUE, FALSE, TRUE, F, T)
typeof(lgl)

## [1] "logical"

print(lgl)

## [1]  TRUE FALSE  TRUE FALSE  TRUE
```

Numeric vector

A numeric vector num is created in Example A.16.

The seq function creates a vector of double type numbers (double-precision numbers).

The double type is proved by the typeof(num) command.

You can see the numbers as shown by the print(num) command.

The number of elements is 40 as displayed by the length(num) command.

Example A.16

```
num <- c(seq(from = 1, to = 100, by = 2.5))
typeof(num)

## [1] "double"

print(num)

##  [1]  1.0  3.5  6.0  8.5 11.0 13.5 16.0 18.5 21.0 23
.5 26.0 28.5 31.0 33.5 36.0
## [16] 38.5 41.0 43.5 46.0 48.5 51.0 53.5 56.0 58.5 61
.0 63.5 66.0 68.5 71.0 73.5
```

```
## [31] 76.0 78.5 81.0 83.5 86.0 88.5 91.0 93.5 96.0 98
.5
```

```
length(num)
```

```
## [1] 40
```

Coercing Element Types

The elements of a vector must all be of the same data types. If they are not, R will try to coerce them into the same data types.

In Example A.17 in grt1, except for the 2nd element, the others are characters. The number 5 is coerced into character. grt1 is a character vector. The number of its elements is three as proved by the length(greeting) command.

Example A.17

```
greeting <- c("R is among the top", 5, "choice for anal
ytics")
print(greeting)
```

```
## [1] "R is among the top"    "5"                   "c
hoice for analytics"
```

```
typeof(greeting)
```

```
## [1] "character"
```

```
length(greeting)
```

```
## [1] 3
```

The elements of a vector are indexed. The index starts at 1, i.e. the index of the first element is 1; the second, 2; the third, 3, and so on. In Example A.18, the vector has 27 elements, their index are 1, 2, ..., 27.

[N] on the Vector Display

When you display the content of a vector, you notice the [1] at the beginning of the output.

Example A.18

```
num1 <- c(seq(from = 1, to = 10, by = 2.5))
print(num1)
```

```
## [1] 1.0 3.5 6.0 8.5
```

While in Example A.18 one line is long enough to display four elements, in Example A.19 three lines are required, as one line can accomodate 19 elements.

Example A.19

```
num <- c(seq(from = 1, to = 100, by = 2.5))
num
```

```
##  [1]  1.0  3.5  6.0  8.5 11.0 13.5 16.0 18.5 21.0 23
.5 26.0 28.5 31.0 33.5 36.0
## [16] 38.5 41.0 43.5 46.0 48.5 51.0 53.5 56.0 58.5 61
.0 63.5 66.0 68.5 71.0 73.5
## [31] 76.0 78.5 81.0 83.5 86.0 88.5 91.0 93.5 96.0 98
.5
```

```
# print(num)
```

The [N] at the begining of the vector display is the index of the element right next to it. Hence, [1] is always on the first line of the vector display. In the example, the [20] on the second line indicates the index of the element next to it is 20.

For the same vector, the subsequent [N] after [1] can be different, they depend on the line size (length), i.e. the number of elements a line can accomodate to display.

num <- c(seq(from = 1, to = 100, by = 2.5)) print(num) [1] 1.0 3.5 6.0 8.5 11.0 13.5 16.0 18.5 21.0 23.5 [11] 26.0 28.5 31.0 33.5 36.0 38.5 41.0 43.5 46.0 48.5 [21] 51.0 53.5 56.0 58.5 61.0 63.5 66.0 68.5 71.0 73.5 [31] 76.0 78.5 81.0 83.5 86.0 88.5 91.0 93.5 96.0 98.5 typeof(num) [1] "double" length(num) [1] 40

Name of Variable

Instead of hw, you can name the variable, for example, helloworld.

Please update hw to helloworld in the two lines and execute the script by pressing **Ctrl+Alt+R**.The output should be exactly the same when helloword was hw.

Example A.20

```
# To get iniated into R
helloworld <- "Hello, World!" # store the greeting in h
w object
print(helloworld)              # print (display) the con
tent of hw object on the console

## [1] "Hello, World!"
```

Name of object must obey the following:

- Don't use reserved words.
  - Some commonly used reserved words are: if, then, function, TRUE, and FALSE.
  - To see the list of reserved words type **help(reserved)** on the Console pane and press Ctrl+Enter to execcute the command. The list of the reserved words are displayed on Help pane.
- Start with a letter (a – z and A to Z), or a dot, but do not followed by a number.
- Follow the first character with letters, numbers, dot, and underline.

Name is Case-sensitive

Name is case-sensitive. helloworld is different from **H**elloworld and hello**W**orld.

Try them. The print on the 2nd line is good. However, the last two commands give you errors, because they try to print the two objects that do not exist.

Example A.21

```
helloworld <- "Hello, World!"
print(helloworld)
```

```
## [1] "Hello, World!"

print(Helloworld)

## Error in print(Helloworld): object 'Helloworld' not
found

print(helloWorld)

## Error in print(helloWorld): object 'helloWorld' not
found
```

While you can create a one element vector, like that in line 2, by assigning (storing) the element ("Hello, World!"), you need to use c(...) to create a vector with more than one element. Line 5 creates a vector with three elements. The first element is ...; second, ...; and third, ...

print(), is.vector() and c() are functions.

hw in print(hw) and in is.vector(hw) is an argument of the functions. Function can have more than one argument, like that in the c(1,2,3) of line ..

Index of Elements

To access vector elements we use index. Index of first element is 1; second, 2; and so on.

To access more than one element, indicate the indeces of the elements you want in a vector. In line 3 we use c(2, 3) to indicate that we want to access the second and third elements.

The command **num3**, just the name of the object, is another way to just display the content of a object.

Example A.22

```
num2 <- c("Ben", "Neeraj", "Linda", "Andy")
num2[1]

## [1] "Ben"
```

```
num2[c(2, 3)]
```

```
## [1] "Neeraj" "Linda"
```

```
num3 <- num2[1:3]
num3
```

```
## [1] "Ben"    "Neeraj" "Linda"
```

Named Elements

Once named, though the index is still available, you can refer the vector elements by their names. In EXample.. the num1's elements are named first, second, and third.

We then access the second element by its name, "second".

To access more than one element, similar to access by indices, indicate the elements you want in a vector. In line 3 we indicate by the **c("first", "third")** that we want to access the the first and the third elements.

The next two lines demonstrate that we can still access by index.

Example A.23

```
num1 <- c(first = 1, second = 2.2, third = 3.33, fourth
= 4.444)
num1["second"]
```

```
## second
##    2.2
```

```
num1[c("first","third")]
```

```
## first third
##  1.00  3.33
```

```
num1[2]
```

```
## second
##    2.2
```

```
num1[c(1, 3)]
```

```
## first third
##  1.00  3.33
```

Dataframe, Factor and List

In addition to vector, two other data structures: dataframe and list, are used in OneR.

Dataframe

A dataframe looks like a table. Data in a dataframe is stored as rows and columns.

You can create a dataframe using **data.frame** function.

In Example A.24 we create a **loss** dataframe that stores seven rows with four columns of data.

claimnumber lossdate claimant payment 111 2019-12-01 Ron 300 112 2019-11-23 Dean 500 113 2020-11-15 Mirna 1000 114 2020-05-11 Dylan 750 115 2020-03-27 Gabbie 800 116 2020-03-27 Amy 800 117 2020-03-27 John 800

Line 1 to 4 construct four vectors. The claimnumber vector stores the seven claimnumbers of the seven rows. We use the other three vectors similary to store the lossdate, claimant and payment columns of the seven rows. Line 5 then constructs the loss dataframe from the four vectors.

The **str(loss)** shows that loss is a dataframe that has 7 obs (rows) and 4 variables (columns). It also shows the structure: the four columns and their data types, as well some samples of the data.

The print(loss) displays the loss dataframe.

Example A.24

```
claimnumber = c (111:117)
lossdate = as.Date(c("2019-12-01", "2019-11-23", "2020-
11-15", "2020-05-11", "2020-03-27", "2020-03-27", "2020
-03-27"))
claimant = c("Ron","Dean","Mirna","Dylan","Gabbie","Amy
","John")
payment = c(300, 500, 1000, 750, 800, 800, 800)
```

```
loss <- data.frame(claimnumber,lossdate,claimant,paymen
t)
str(loss)

## 'data.frame':    7 obs. of  4 variables:
##  $ claimnumber: int  111 112 113 114 115 116 117
##  $ lossdate   : Date, format: "2019-12-01" "2019-11-
23" ...
##  $ claimant   : Factor w/ 7 levels "Amy","Dean","Dyl
an",..: 7 2 6 3 4 1 5
##  $ payment    : num  300 500 1000 750 800 800 800

print(loss)

##   claimnumber   lossdate claimant payment
## 1         111 2019-12-01      Ron     300
## 2         112 2019-11-23     Dean     500
## 3         113 2020-11-15    Mirna    1000
## 4         114 2020-05-11    Dylan     750
## 5         115 2020-03-27   Gabbie     800
## 6         116 2020-03-27      Amy     800
## 7         117 2020-03-27     John     800
```

Importing Dataframe

Often you import dataframe from a file, such as csv file.

Example A.25 calls the **read.csv** function to import creditcard_upgrade_history.csv file and stores the dataframe in a variable named ccuhd.

Here is the creditcard_upgrade_history.csv file that we used in Chapter 1. Note that the first row has the column headings (column names)

Travel,Family,Work,Card,Income,Upgrade
Rare,Kids,Sales,Silver,100000,No
Rare,Kids,Sales,Gold,125000,No
Frequent,Kids,Sales,Silver,150000,Yes
Occasional,Single,Sales,Silver,150000,Yes
Occasional,Couple,Office,Silver,150000,Yes
Occasional,Couple,Office,Gold,125000,No

Frequent,Couple,Office,Silver,100000,Yes
Rare,Single,Sales,Silver,100000,No
Frequent,Couple,Office,Silver,150000,Yes
Occasional,Single,Office,Silver,125000,Yes
Rare,Single,Office,Gold,150000,Yes
Frequent,Single,Sales,Silver,150000,Yes
Frequent,Kids,Office,Silver,100000,Yes
Occasional,Single,Sales,Silver,150000,No

Example A.25

```
ccuhd <- read.csv("C:/OneR/creditcard_upgrade_history.c
sv") [, c (2:7)]
print(ccuhd)
```

```
##           Travel Family   Work   Card Income Upgrade
## 1           Rare   Kids  Sales Silver 100000      No
## 2           Rare   Kids  Sales   Gold 110000      No
## 3       Frequent   Kids  Sales Silver 120000     Yes
## 4     Occasional Single  Sales Silver 120000     Yes
## 5     Occasional Couple Office Silver 120000     Yes
## 6     Occasional Couple Office   Gold 150000      No
## 7       Frequent Couple Office Silver 100000     Yes
## 8           Rare Single  Sales Silver 100000      No
## 9       Frequent Couple Office Silver 100000     Yes
## 10    Occasional Single Office Silver 130000     Yes
## 11          Rare Single Office   Gold 150000     Yes
## 12      Frequent Single  Sales Silver 100000     Yes
## 13      Frequent   Kids Office Silver 110000     Yes
## 14    Occasional Single  Sales Silver 110000      No
```

Accessing rows and columns

You can access the rows of a data frame using row numbers. The syntax is as follows. Note that you need a comma after the last rownumber.

dataframe[rownumber1, rownumber2, ... lastrownumber,]

Example A.26 accesses row number 5 of the df1 dataframe.

Example A.26

```
ccuhd[5,]
```

```
##        Travel Family    Work   Card Income Upgrade
## 5 Occasional Couple Office Silver 120000     Yes
```

Example A.27 accesses row numbers 1, 2, and 3. The **1:3** generates a sequence of three numbers from 1 to 3 with 1 increments, essentially a vector with three elements: 1, 2 and 3.

Example A.27

```
ccuhd[1:3,]
```

```
##       Travel Family  Work   Card Income Upgrade
## 1       Rare   Kids Sales Silver 100000      No
## 2       Rare   Kids Sales   Gold 110000      No
## 3 Frequent   Kids Sales Silver 120000     Yes
```

Example A.28 accesses row numbers 1 and 3, and 10 to 15. The innermost c function creates a vector of two elements. The outer c function creates a vector

Example A.28

```
ccuhd[ (c(c(1, 3), 10:15)), ]
```

```
##         Travel Family   Work   Card Income Upgrade
## 1          Rare   Kids  Sales Silver 100000      No
## 3      Frequent   Kids  Sales Silver 120000     Yes
## 10 Occasional Single Office Silver 130000     Yes
## 11         Rare Single Office   Gold 150000     Yes
## 12   Frequent Single  Sales Silver 100000     Yes
## 13   Frequent   Kids Office Silver 110000     Yes
## 14 Occasional Single  Sales Silver 110000      No
## NA        <NA>   <NA>   <NA>   <NA>     NA    <NA>
```

How about accessing specific columns?

You can use column names.

Example . access row 1 to 3 and only columns: Card and Family.

Example A.29

```
ccuhd[1:3, c("Card","Family")]
```

```
##       Card Family
## 1 Silver   Kids
## 2   Gold   Kids
## 3 Silver   Kids
```

Factor

A factor stores data as indexes that represent elements of a
vector.

In Example A.30 the c() function creates the family profiles of
eight card holders. The factor() function converts the vector into
a factor. The is.factor() proves that family_fac is indeed a factor.

the str() function shows that Family_fac is a factor with 3 levels:
"Couple',"Kids" and "Single", the distinct elements of the Family
vector elements. The elements are stored as indexes that
represent the three levels. 1 represents "Kids"; 2, "Single;
3,"Couple". The first element is"Kids", hence the index is 2;
second element"Single", index is 3; and so on.

Example A.30

```
family <- c('Kids','Single','Couple','Couple','Single',
'Couple','Kids')
family_fac <- factor(family)
is.factor(family_fac)
```

```
## [1] TRUE
```

```
str(family_fac)
```

```
##  Factor w/ 3 levels "Couple","Kids",..: 2 3 1 1 3 1
2
```

Numeric factor

We convert numeric vector to a factor by calling cut() function.

In Example A.31 the num_fac numeric vector has 16 elements shown by the print(s). The cut(s) with break = 4 converts s into a factor with four levels.

Notice the notation of the factor levels **(range]**, where range = start, end.

Example A.31

```
num <- seq(from = 20, to = 50, by = 2)
print(num)
```

```
##  [1] 20 22 24 26 28 30 32 34 36 38 40 42 44 46 48 50
```

```
num_fac <- cut(num, breaks = 4)
str(num_fac)
```

```
##  Factor w/ 4 levels "(20,27.5]","(27.5,35]",..: 1 1
## 1 1 2 2 2 2 3 3 ...
```

```
print(num_fac)
```

```
##  [1] (20,27.5] (20,27.5] (20,27.5] (20,27.5] (27.5,3
## 5] (27.5,35] (27.5,35]
##  [8] (27.5,35] (35,42.5] (35,42.5] (35,42.5] (35,42.
## 5] (42.5,50] (42.5,50]
## [15] (42.5,50] (42.5,50]
## Levels: (20,27.5] (27.5,35] (35,42.5] (42.5,50]
```

We can label the levels. The labels give the numeric ranges some names.

In Example A.32 the four numeric labels are now "Low", "MidLow", "MidHigh" and "High". Index 1 is for Low; 2 for MidLow; 3 for MidHigh and 4 for High.

Example A.32

```
num <- seq(from = 20, to = 50, by = 2)
print(num)
```

```
##  [1] 20 22 24 26 28 30 32 34 36 38 40 42 44 46 48 50
```

```r
num_fac <- cut(num, breaks = 4, labels = c("Low","MidLow", "MidHigh","High"), ordered_resulst = TRUE )
str(num_fac)
```

```
##  Factor w/ 4 levels "Low","MidLow",..: 1 1 1 1 2 2 2 2 3 3 ...
```

```r
print(num_fac)
```

```
##  [1] Low      Low      Low      Low      MidLow   MidLow
MidLow   MidLow   MidHigh
## [10] MidHigh MidHigh MidHigh High     High     High
High
## Levels: Low MidLow MidHigh High
```

List

While all elements in a vector must have the same data type, list can have elements with different data types.

You create a list by calling the list() function. You pass the elements you want the list to store in the arguments.

The list1 list in Example A.33 has three elements. The elements have different data types: number, character and logical.

str function shows the structure and data type of the elements.

Example A.33

```
list1 <- list(1, "One", TRUE)
str(list1)

## List of 3
##  $ : num 1
##  $ : chr "One"
##  $ : logi TRUE
```

List a very flexible data structure in terms of the varierty of data it can store.

list2 in Example A.34 stores a numeric vector, a logical vector, a list, and even a dataframe.

Example A.34

```
list2 <- list(c(1, 20, 30), c(TRUE, F), list1, ccuhd)
str(list2)

## List of 4
##  $ : num [1:3] 1 20 30
##  $ : logi [1:2] TRUE FALSE
##  $ :List of 3
##   ..$ : num 1
##   ..$ : chr "One"
##   ..$ : logi TRUE
##  $ :'data.frame':    14 obs. of  6 variables:
##   ..$ Travel : Factor w/ 3 levels "Frequent","Occasi
```

```
onal",..: 3 3 1 2 2 2 1 3 1 2 ...
##   ..$ Family : Factor w/ 3 levels "Couple","Kids",..
: 2 2 2 3 1 1 1 3 1 3 ...
##   ..$ Work   : Factor w/ 2 levels "Office","Sales":
2 2 2 2 1 1 1 2 1 1 ...
##   ..$ Card   : Factor w/ 2 levels "Gold","Silver": 2
1 2 2 2 1 2 2 2 2 ...
##   ..$ Income : int [1:14] 100000 110000 120000 12000
0 120000 150000 100000 100000 100000 130000 ...
##   ..$ Upgrade: Factor w/ 2 levels "No","Yes": 1 1 2
2 2 1 2 1 2 2 ...
```

The model created by OneR is actually a list. The is.list(ccuorm) proves that ccuorm is a list. The str(ccuorm) command shows the structure of the list and some samples of its content.

Example A.35

```
library(OneR)
ccd <- read.csv("C:/OneR/creditcard.csv")
ccuorm <- OneR(ccd)
is.list(ccuorm)

## [1] TRUE

str(ccuorm)

## List of 7
## $ call              : language OneR.data.frame(x = c
cd)
## $ target            : chr "Upgrade"
## $ feature           : chr "Member"
## $ rules             :List of 14
##   ..$ Adrian   : chr "Yes"
##   ..$ Amber    : chr "No"
##   ..$ Christie: chr "No"
##   ..$ Daren    : chr "Yes"
##   ..$ Florence: chr "Yes"
##   ..$ Gus      : chr "Yes"
##   ..$ Katie    : chr "No"
##   ..$ Pamela   : chr "Yes"
##   ..$ Sharon   : chr "Yes"
##   ..$ Ulma     : chr "Yes"
```

```
##    ..$ Vinnie  : chr "Yes"
##    ..$ Wesley  : chr "Yes"
##    ..$ Yan     : chr "No"
##    ..$ Zach    : chr "No"
##  $ correct_instances: num 14
##  $ total_instances  : int 14
##  $ cont_table       : 'table' int [1:2, 1:14] 0 1 1
0 1 0 0 1 0 1 ...
##    ..- attr(*, "dimnames")=List of 2
##    .. ..$ Upgrade: chr [1:2] "No" "Yes"
##    .. ..$ Member : chr [1:14] "Adrian" "Amber" "Chris
tie" "Daren" ...
##  - attr(*, "class")= chr "OneR"
```